CITIES OF EUROPE

LIZ GOGERLY

**ILLUSTRATED BY
VICTOR BEUREN**

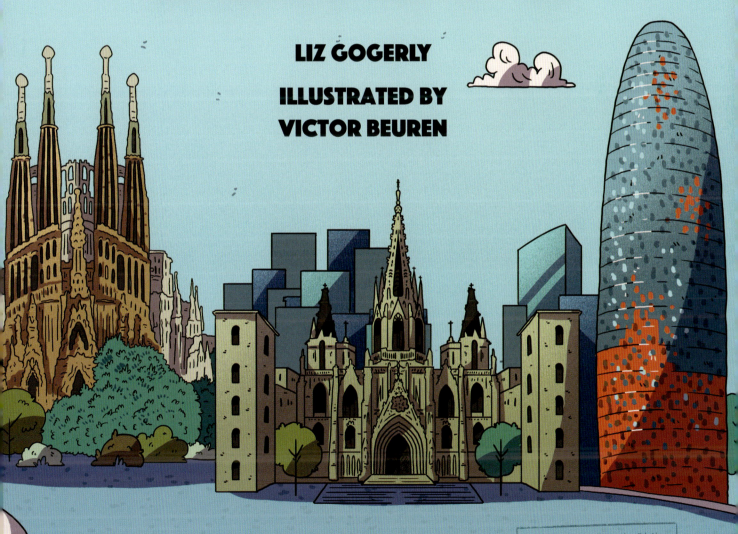

W
FRANKLIN WATTS
LONDON•SYDNEY

Franklin Watts
First published in Great Britain in 2021
by The Watts Publishing Group

Credits
Artwork by Victor Beuren
Design: Collaborate Agency
Editor: Nicola Edwards

ISBN 978 1 4451 6850 0 (hb); 978 1 4451 6851 7 (pb)

Printed in Dubai

Franklin Watts
An imprint of
Hachette Children's Group
Part of the Watts Publishing Group
Carmelite House
50 Victoria Embankment
London EC4Y 0DZ

An Hachette UK Company
www.hachette.co.uk

www.franklinwatts.co.uk

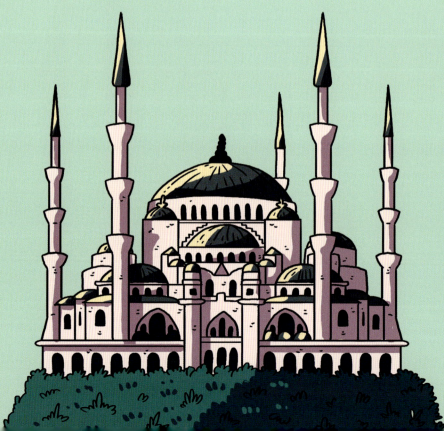

CONTENTS

CITIES OF EUROPE

Europe is filled with fascinating cities of all shapes, sizes and ages. Andorra la Vella, in the Pyrenees between Spain and France, at , 1,050 m altitude is the highest capital in Europe. With around 15 million people, Istanbul in Turkey is the biggest city in terms of population. Europe's oldest city is Plovdiv in Bulgaria (right), which dates back to around 6000 BCE. Athens, the next oldest, was founded in about 3000 BCE.

Europe is the sixth-smallest of the seven continents. It has a population of around 741.4 million which makes it the fourth most populated continent after Asia, Africa and the Americas.

Europe has 51 countries – including independent states and transcontinental (located in two or more continents) states. Most experts list the top three biggest cities by population size as Istanbul, Moscow, with around 12 million people, and London, with about 9 million.

The skyline of many European cities has changed dramatically in the last century, with more and more tall buildings going up since the 1990s. Istanbul, Moscow and London have the most skyscrapers over 150 m tall in Europe. The Lakhta Center in St Petersburg in Russia stands at 462.5 m, making it the tallest building in Europe. Federation Tower in Moscow comes second at 373.7 m. OKO: South Tower in Moscow is third at 354.1 m.

OKO: South Tower

Lakhta Center

Federation Tower

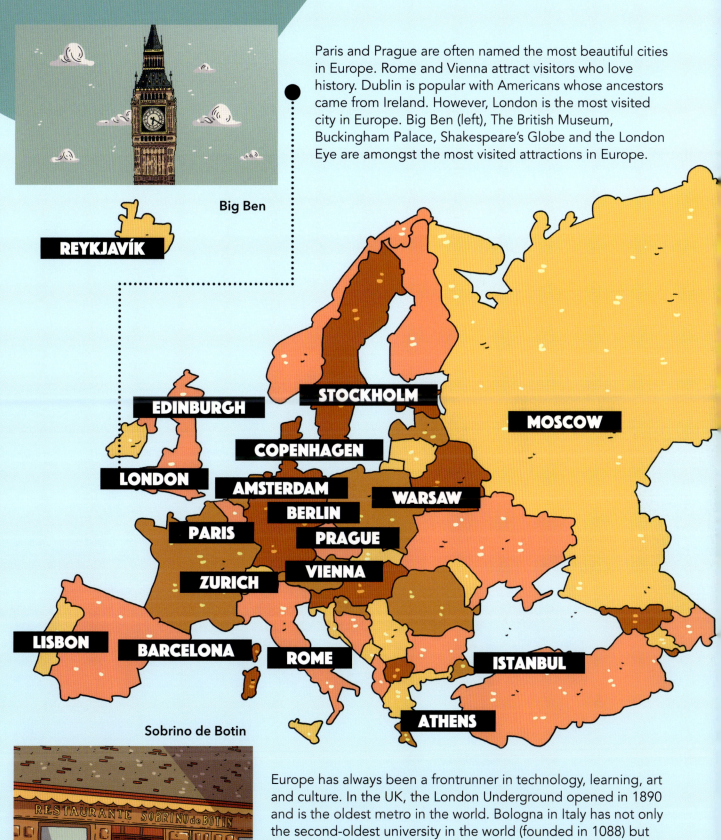

Paris and Prague are often named the most beautiful cities in Europe. Rome and Vienna attract visitors who love history. Dublin is popular with Americans whose ancestors came from Ireland. However, London is the most visited city in Europe. Big Ben (left), The British Museum, Buckingham Palace, Shakespeare's Globe and the London Eye are amongst the most visited attractions in Europe.

Big Ben

REYKJAVÍK

EDINBURGH

STOCKHOLM

MOSCOW

COPENHAGEN

LONDON

AMSTERDAM

BERLIN

WARSAW

PARIS

PRAGUE

ZURICH

VIENNA

LISBON

BARCELONA

ROME

ISTANBUL

ATHENS

Sobrino de Botin

Europe has always been a frontrunner in technology, learning, art and culture. In the UK, the London Underground opened in 1890 and is the oldest metro in the world. Bologna in Italy has not only the second-oldest university in the world (founded in 1088) but possibly the oldest art school. In Madrid, Spain, you'll find Sobrino de Botin (left), which is claimed to be the world's oldest restaurant!

So pack your bags and don't forget your passport, as we explore some of the most amazing cities in Europe.

Federation Tower

You can zoom up to the observation deck of the main skyscraper of the Federation Tower to get an awesome view over the city. This impressive structure actually has two towers. The taller East Tower measures 374 m at its top floor and 450 m at its antenna spire.

The Ostankino Tower

Moscow may not have the highest skyscraper in Europe (see page 4) but it does have the tallest structure. The Ostankino Tower is a 540.1-m-tall television and radio mast with a 334-m-high restaurant called 7th Heaven.

Red Square

The State Historical Museum stands at one end of Red Square (Krasnaya Ploshchad)

The Moscow River

The Moscow River (Moskva River) passes right through the centre of the city. If you take a boat trip up the river, you can see the mighty towers of the Kremlin up close.

St. Basil's

St. Basil's Cathedral is one of the most famous buildings in the world. You can't miss it – the multi-coloured domes look like Christmas decorations. It was built in the sixteenth century by the first tsar of Russia, Ivan the Terrible.

MOSCOW
RUSSIA

Welcome to Moscow, the capital of Russia and the biggest city in the country with a population of around 13.2 million. This is a city of contrasts – hot summers and cold winters with tonnes of snow. Moscow is famous for its beautiful historic buildings but also has many modern structures, including the second highest skyscraper in Europe.

Kremlin
The Moscow Kremlin is a red-walled fortress beside the Moscow River. Inside the walls here are five cathedrals and many beautiful old buildings and towers. The President of Russia lives in the Grand Kremlin Palace.

Archangel Cathedral
The Archangel Cathedral is inside the Moscow Kremlin. It was built between 1505 and 1508 and, with its five shining domes of gold and silver, it shimmers in the sunshine.

Moscow Metro
If you want to get round this city quickly then jump on the Moscow Metro. This is the busiest underground in Europe and possibly the most beautiful. Many of its stunning stations have marble walls, mosaics and impressive chandeliers.

HISTORY

Moscow became the capital of parts of Russia back in the fourteenth century. At this time the city was centred around the Moscow Kremlin. In 1713, the capital was moved to St Petersburg but Moscow continued to grow. After the Russian Revolution of 1917, Moscow became the capital city once more, this time of the communist Soviet Russia.

Rouble (or ruble) notes and kopek coins are the currency here.

MONEY

Lenin's Mausoleum

PLACES TO GO

The Old Arbat

The Old Arbat is in the centre of the city and has a history going back to the fifteenth century. Many famous Russian artists and writers, such as the poets Alexander Pushkin and Marina Tsvetaeva, lived here. Today it has upmarket shops, beautiful chapels and churches to explore.

Lenin's Mausoleum on Red Square

Visit Lenin's Mausoleum on Red Square to pay your respects to the Russian revolutionary and leader of Soviet Russia. His body has been embalmed and laid to rest for everyone to see.

Bolshoi Theatre

Book to see the ballet or opera at the historic Bolshoi Theatre. The Bolshoi Ballet and Bolshoi Opera regularly perform on this famous stage. Tchaikovsky's ballet *Swan Lake* was first danced here in 1877.

GUM

Moscow is one of the most expensive cities in the world. You would need thousands of roubles to shop at the luxury State Department Store (also known as GUM) on Red Square. Muscovites (the name for people who live in Moscow) say it's more like a museum than a shop!

 # FOOD

Beetroot soup

Borscht soup is a purple soup made from beetroot. In the summer it is served cold, so it's a good way to cool down. However, on a freezing-cold Russian night, there is nothing like a hot bowl of borscht to warm you up!

'Herring under a fur coat'

'Herring under a fur coat' is another classic dish to try in Moscow. Actually, the 'fur coat' is just the salad and vegetables that cover the herring.

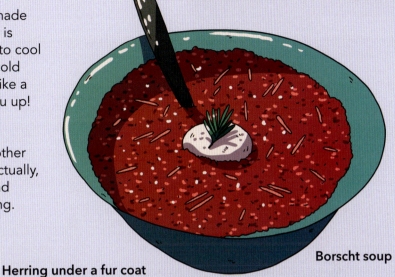

Borscht soup

Herring under a fur coat

 # THINGS TO DO

Experience Moscow's parks

Moscow has more green spaces than any other city in Russia. Gorky Park was opened in 1928 and is the most popular place to relax. All the parks have something to offer, such as open-air cinemas, amusement rides, ice skating rinks, boating lakes, art pavilions, music fountains and rope walks. Moscow's Izmailovsky Park is like a beautiful forest within the city.

Gorky Park

The Seine River winds its way through the heart of the city for about 13 km. It divides the city into the 'Left Bank' and 'Right Bank'. The water may look a sludgy green in places but it is said that 50 per cent of the drinking water in Paris comes from the Seine.

The Eiffel Tower or 'Iron Lady' has dominated the Paris skyline since it was completed in 1889. It was the tallest tower in the world until 1930 and at its tip it measures 324 m. People can visit the 276-m-high observation deck for the best views over the city. Every night for five minutes each hour the lights of the Eiffel Tower sparkle like magic and lasers are beamed up into the night air.

Notre Dame is the famous Gothic cathedral that stands at the very centre of the city. It's over 850 years old but many of its beautiful features, such as its spire and the sculptures of the Twelve Apostles, were added in the nineteenth century. In April 2019 the roof of the cathedral caught fire and parts of the building were destroyed.

There are 37 bridges spanning the Seine in Paris. The **Pont Neuf** is the oldest, although its name actually means 'new bridge'. The bridge was completed in 1607 and has a total of 12 arches connecting the Right and Left Banks.

PARIS

FRANCE

Bonjour and have a wonderful stay in Paris! The French capital has earned the name 'City of Love' for its beauty and popularity with couples looking for a romantic holiday. It is also known as the 'City of Light' because it was one of the first cities to switch to gas street lighting. If you love fashion, food and art then Paris is for you! It has a population of around 2.1 million and its citizens are known as Parisians (*Parisiens* in French).

The Arc de Triomphe was built to honour the soldiers that had died in the Napoleonic Wars (1803-1815). Underneath its arch is the Tomb of the Unknown Soldier which symbolises those who lost their lives in the First and Second World Wars. Since 1923 an eternal flame on top of the tomb has burned in their memory.

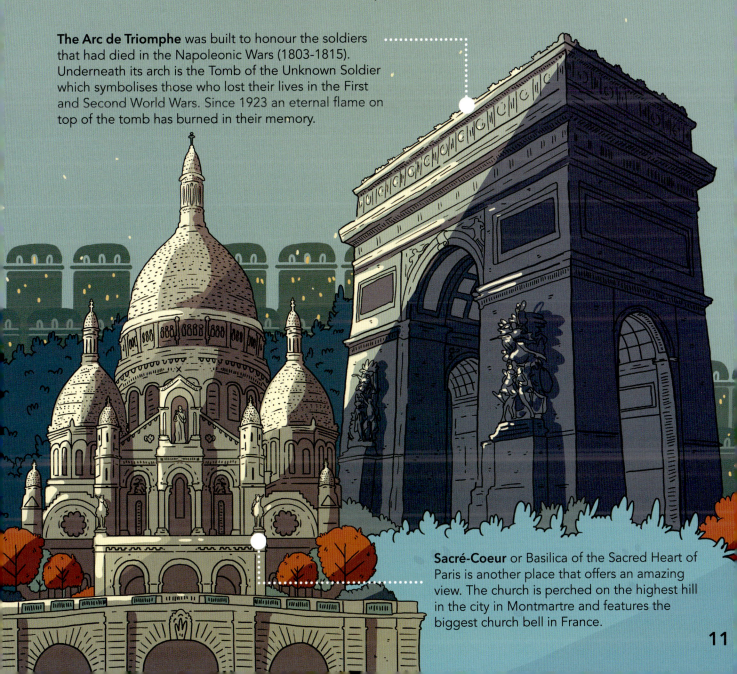

Sacré-Coeur or Basilica of the Sacred Heart of Paris is another place that offers an amazing view. The church is perched on the highest hill in the city in Montmartre and features the biggest church bell in France.

HISTORY

Paris was founded on the banks of the Seine in the third century BCE by fishermen called the Parisii. In its time, Paris has been the scene for revolution, occupation and liberation. Many of the wide boulevards and grand buildings we see today were begun in the nineteenth century. This was also an exciting time in art, literature and fashion. Paris became a hub for artists including Monet, Degas, Picasso and Dalí. Writers from overseas such as Henry Miller and Ernest Hemingway settled here for a while. Paris fashion set the trends around the world. Explore this beautiful city and its rich history begins to unfold.

MONEY

The French franc was the official currency in France until 1999, when many countries in the European Union began using the Euro.

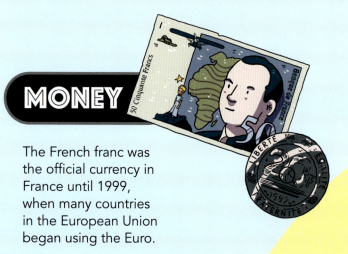

THINGS TO DO

Ride the Batobus

One of the best ways to see all the major landmarks in the city is to take the Batobus which is like a bus, but it's a boat! These boats have glass walls and roofs so you'll get a great view of Notre Dame, the Louvre, the Grand Palais and the Eiffel Tower.

Go to the beach!

Seriously, since 2002 Paris has its very own beach on the Right Bank of the Seine near the Pont Neuf. It may be artificial but in the summer months it gets very crowded.

Shop until you drop!

Paris is the home of couture, or high fashion. Designers like Christian Dior and Coco Chanel started their labels here. Head to the Champs-Élysées for fancy designer boutiques and all the top brands.

Batobus

FOOD

Chocolate

Paris is home to some of the top chocolatiers (makers of chocolate) on the planet. The best chocolate in Paris doesn't come wrapped in bars, it is displayed in cabinets like works of art. Caramel and fruit are smothered in delicious chocolate. Meanwhile, chocolate is melted and served with hot milk to create the dreamiest hot chocolate ever.

Pain au chocolat

Anyone for more chocolate? Then don't forget to try a *pain au chocolat* (croissant with chunks of chocolate). You'll find these tasty treats at a *patisserie* (pastry shop) or *boulangerie* (bakery).

Clignancourt flea market

PLACES TO GO

The Porte de Clignancourt flea market

Clignancourt flea market (also called Les Puces which translates as 'the Fleas') is the biggest antique market in the world with around 11 million visitors each year.

The Louvre

The Louvre is the largest museum in the world, with around 13 km of corridors! It has over 380,000 objects and 35,000 works of art, including the 'Mona Lisa' by Leonardo da Vinci. People have been admiring that famous smile since the portrait was first displayed here in 1804.

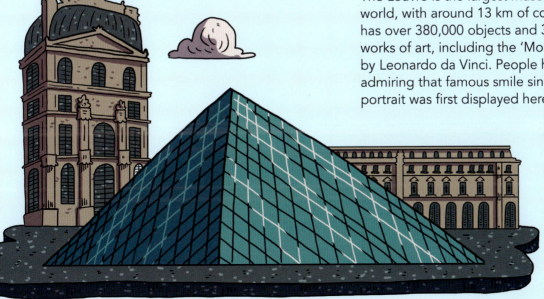

The Louvre

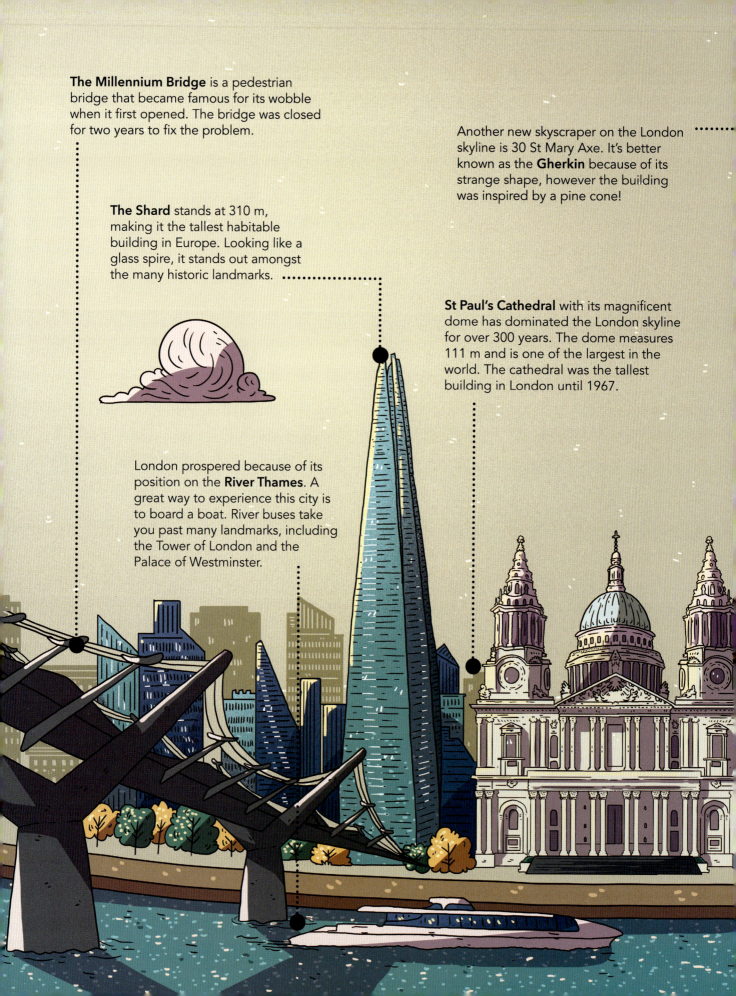

The Millennium Bridge is a pedestrian bridge that became famous for its wobble when it first opened. The bridge was closed for two years to fix the problem.

Another new skyscraper on the London skyline is 30 St Mary Axe. It's better known as the **Gherkin** because of its strange shape, however the building was inspired by a pine cone!

The Shard stands at 310 m, making it the tallest habitable building in Europe. Looking like a glass spire, it stands out amongst the many historic landmarks.

St Paul's Cathedral with its magnificent dome has dominated the London skyline for over 300 years. The dome measures 111 m and is one of the largest in the world. The cathedral was the tallest building in London until 1967.

London prospered because of its position on the **River Thames**. A great way to experience this city is to board a boat. River buses take you past many landmarks, including the Tower of London and the Palace of Westminster.

LONDON
UNITED KINGDOM

London is one of the oldest and largest cities in Europe. The capital of Britain has an estimated population of around 9 million and in the past earned the nicknames the 'Big Smoke' and the 'Swinging City'. History hits you at every turn in London with some of the most iconic buildings in the world. It's still a swinging place with food, fashion, art and music very much alive and kicking!

Many new buildings were erected to celebrate the new millennium. In 2000, the **Millennium Dome** was opened, housing a large exhibition. Today, it is better known as The O2 and it hosts shows and concerts.

There are 35 bridges that cross the River Thames in London. **Tower Bridge** is one of the most famous. It was opened in 1894.

On the banks of the Thames stands the mighty **Tower of London**. This famous royal castle (and former prison and execution site!) dates back to 1078. Today, it houses the British Crown Jewels.

15

HISTORY

In about 50 CE, the Romans built a bridge across a narrow part of the Thames, and started a settlement they called Londinium. Later the Romans made it their capital. In 1066, William I built the palace he called the Tower of London and the city continued to grow into one of the biggest in Europe. The River Thames has always been at the heart of the city's success, bringing trade, industry, finance and power to the capital. By Victorian times (1837-1901), London was the centre of world trade. London suffered terribly in the Second World War (1939-1945), but in the twenty-first century the city continues to thrive and attract visitors from around the world.

Tower Bridge

Elizabeth II

MONEY

The official currency is the pound sterling. All the notes feature the Queen's head.

PLACES TO GO

London's museums

There are more than 170 museums in London and many of them are free to visit. The British Museum opened in 1759 and has millions of ancient and historical artefacts from all over the world. The Natural History Museum explores the plant and animal kingdoms – watch out for the realistic animatronic dinosaurs! The Victoria and Albert Museum has the largest collections covering art, fashion and design in the world.

Buckingham Palace

You won't be able to say 'hello' to the Queen, but in the summer Buckingham Palace opens its doors to the public and you can peek inside 19 of its state rooms (there are 775 rooms in total).

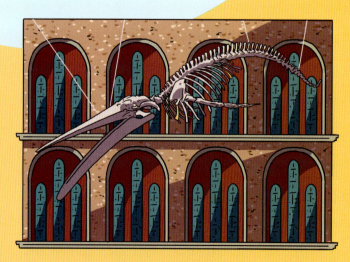

Natural History Museum

FOOD

London is home to people from many backgrounds and cultures. This is reflected in the wide selection of food on offer.

However, if you're searching for something more traditional, there are still a few **pie and mash** shops as well as plenty of places selling **fish and chips**. **Jellied eels** is another old-fashioned dish which dates from the eighteenth century.

Pie and mash with parsley liquor

Platform 9¾

THINGS TO DO

Visit Platform 9 ¾

Harry Potter fans can visit Platform 9 ¾ at Kings Cross Station. You won't be able to board the Hogwarts Express but you can take a great photograph!

Take a trip on a double decker

Ding Ding! Jump aboard a double decker, open-top bus for a trip around the city. Some companies offer special tours but some of the local buses go on similar routes. This is a great way to see sites including the Tower of London, Big Ben, Trafalgar Square and the Houses of Parliament.

Ride in the London Eye

The London Eye on the South Bank of the River Thames was opened in 2000 and has become one of the city's favourite attractions. Take a ride in one of its capsules for far-reaching views over the city.

Double decker bus

To get a bird's eye view across the capital, head to the **Berlin TV Tower** (also called Berliner Fernsehturm). The tower is 368 m high with an observation platform at 200 m. There's a cool, revolving restaurant in the sphere in the middle.

The **Reichstag** building looks truly impressive. This is where the parliament of Germany met until 1933. This was the year that Adolf Hitler became Chancellor of Germany and the Reichstag was set on fire. The building was restored in 1990 after German reunification.

The **large glass dome** of the Reichstag floods the building with natural light. It was designed by the British architect **Norman Foster** and was completed in 1999.

The **Brandenburg Gate** was built in 1791 and is one of the most historic landmarks in Berlin. So much of Berlin was destroyed in the Second World War, but the Brandenburg Gate survived. It is a symbol of freedom and unification for the city.

Berlin is famous for its green spaces. **Grosser Tiergarten** is the largest and oldest park in the city. In the middle of the park stands the **Victory Column (Siegessäule)**. A bronze statue of Victoria, the Roman goddess of Victory, looks over the park.

Berlin has grown along the banks of the River Spree. If you take a **river cruise**, you'll be able to see some of the city's finest landmarks.

BERLIN
GERMANY

Berlin Cathedral was badly damaged during the Second World War, but it was rebuilt in 1975. It's called a cathedral although technically it's a church, as it doesn't have its own bishop! You can get another great view of the city here.

Guten Tag! from Berlin, the capital of Germany. This cosmopolitan city has a population of around 3.7 million. There's something for everyone: stunning historic and modern buildings; a buzzing arts and music scene; and beautiful parks, forests and lakes for swimming and other outdoor pursuits.

At the centre of Berlin is the modern **Potsdamer Platz**. This area was destroyed in the Second World War, but in recent years a cluster of interesting new buildings have sprung up. These are filled with shopping malls, museums and restaurants and attract many visitors to the area.

HISTORY

Berlin was founded in the thirteenth century but it wasn't until the eighteenth century that the city began to grow. By 1871 Berlin was the capital of Germany. In the twentieth century, the city was beset with revolution and war. After the Second World War, much of the city was in ruins. Between 1961 and 1989 the Berlin Wall was erected to divide East Berlin (part of communist East Germany) and West Berlin. Anyone who attempted to escape East Germany by crossing the Berlin Wall was shot. After the collapse of communism, the wall was demolished and Berlin was named the capital of the newly unified Germany.

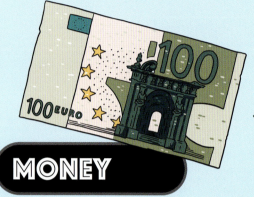

MONEY

The Euro has been the official currency in Germany since 2002.

THINGS TO DO

Visit the Berlin Wall Memorial

At the Berlin Wall Memorial, you can see a part of the original concrete wall. The wall measured 3.6 m high and ran for 43 km through the city. The people living in East Berlin were governed by the Communist Party, which had strict rules about housing, jobs, religion and culture – the tall stark wall seemed to express the repression they felt. Meanwhile in West Berlin the government was democratically elected and people felt freer to live their lives. This was reflected in the graffiti demanding peace and freedom that was scrawled on the west side of the wall. This small section gives us a glimpse of how the wall divided the city.

FOOD

In Germany you'll always find sausages **(wurst)** on the menu. In Berlin the speciality is **currywurst**! It's a sausage served up with a special curry sauce made from tomato ketchup, **Worcestershire sauce** and **curry powder**. Another favourite dish is **schnitzel**, made from thin slices of meat fried in breadcrumbs.

Wurst

Museum Island

PLACES TO GO

Museum Island

Berlin has over 180 amazing museums to explore. On Museum Island, in the Spree River, you can see five of them, including the Pergamon Museum, with its ancient artefacts, and the Old National Gallery, with paintings by famous artists such as Renoir and Monet.

The Memorial to the Murdered Jews of Europe

The Holocaust is a part of history that must never be forgotten. During the Second World War, millions of people were murdered by the Nazis and many of these victims came from Berlin. The Memorial to the Murdered Jews of Europe was opened in central Berlin in 2004. The memorial is made up from 2,711 slabs of concrete that look rather like gravestones in a cemetery.

Memorial to the Murdered Jews of Europe

The city hosted the **Olympic Games in 1992** and it's been growing upwards ever since. These days Barcelona is famed for its skyscrapers, many of which were built for the Games.

Olympic Port and many of the beaches in Barcelona were also created especially for the Barcelona Olympic Games. Barceloneta beach and Nova Icària beach have long stretches of golden sands.

Another eye-catching skyscraper is **W Barcelona**, which looks out to sea. It houses a 99-m-high luxury hotel.

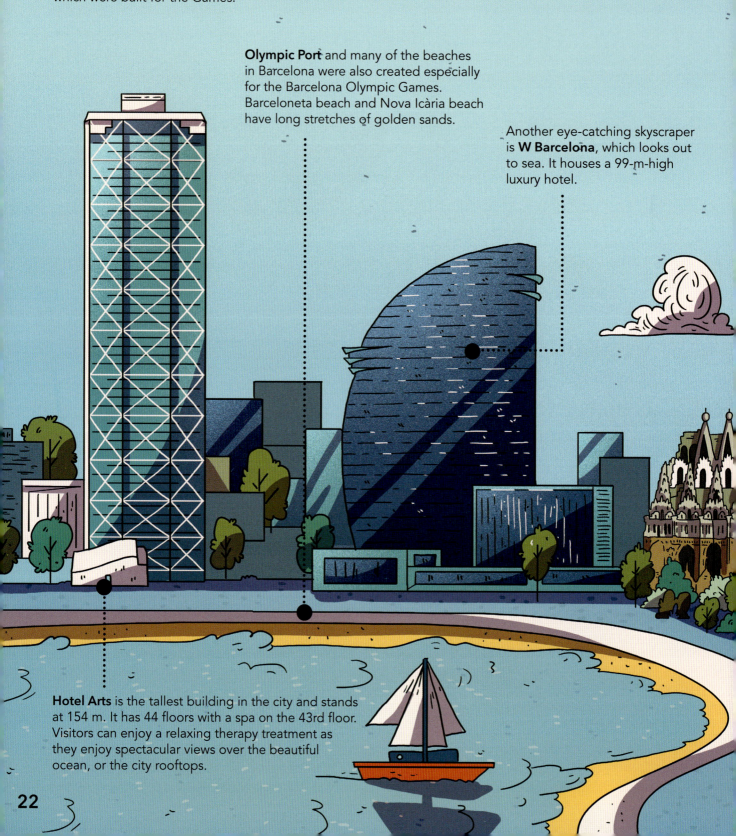

Hotel Arts is the tallest building in the city and stands at 154 m. It has 44 floors with a spa on the 43rd floor. Visitors can enjoy a relaxing therapy treatment as they enjoy spectacular views over the beautiful ocean, or the city rooftops.

BARCELONA
SPAIN

Hola from Barcelona, the Catalan capital. It has a population of around 1.6 million, making it the second most populated city in Spain. Barcelona is situated by the Mediterranean Sea, but it's so much more than a seaside resort. Get your walking shoes on and you'll see some incredible historic buildings, modernist architecture and impressive skyscrapers. And, while you're at it, enjoy the friendly, relaxed atmosphere of this popular city.

In the middle of the city, the unusual-looking **Torre Agbar** has been renamed the **Torre Glòries** (Glòries Tower). It has gained lots of interesting nicknames, based on its shape, but the architect has said he was inspired by the local Montserrat mountains! It is 144 m tall and was opened in 2005.

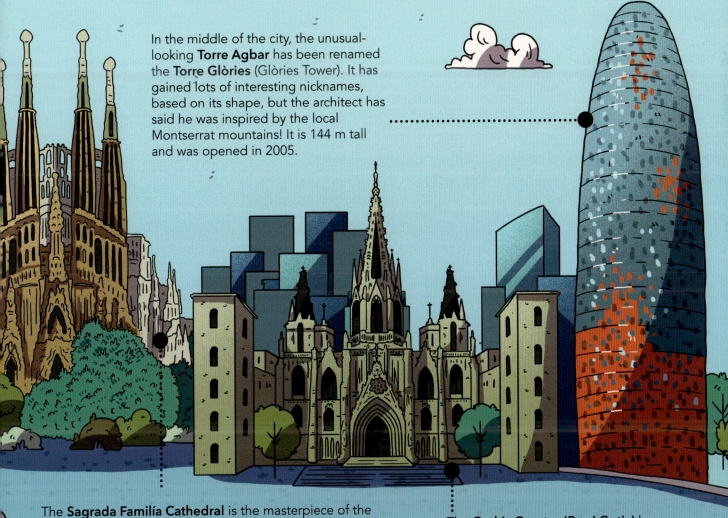

The **Sagrada Família Cathedral** is the masterpiece of the great Catalan architect Antoni Gaudí (1852-1926). Building started here in 1866 but Gaudí took over from 1883 to 1926. He didn't like straight lines or convention so he added curves and colours to his building. It still isn't finished yet but it is one of the most visited buildings in the world!

The **Gothic Quarter (Barri Gotic)** has a maze of narrow old streets and interesting old buildings to explore. At its heart is the Gothic Cathedral which was built between the thirteenth and fifteenth centuries.

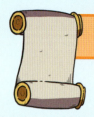

HISTORY

This is a city full of history and culture. It began when the Romans founded the city towards the end of the first century BCE – you can see parts of the walls they built in the Gothic Quarter. Barcelona really began to flourish in the eleventh century, when it became a centre of trade and politics in Europe. In the nineteenth century Catalan architects such as Gaudí and Montaner left their unique marks on the city they loved. In the twentieth century, the city experienced another growth spurt when it hosted the Olympic Games.

Park Güell

MONEY

The currency in Spain is the Euro.

THINGS TO DO

Take in the view from Park Güell

One of the best places to visit with views across the entire city is the terrace at the Parc Güell. This public park was the vision of the architect Antoni Gaudí in 1900. Today, tourists flock here to admire Gaudí's quirky and colourful buildings, mosaics and sculptures.

Visit the Parc de la Ciutadella

The Parc de la Ciutadella is the largest green space in the city. Barcelona Zoo is here and so is the beautiful Cascada fountain which is modelled on the famous Trevi Fountain in Rome (see page 29).

Watch football at Camp Nou

Football fans from all over the world head to Camp Nou, the home stadium for FC Barcelona. It can hold crowds of 99,354 people and is the largest stadium in Europe and the third biggest in the world.

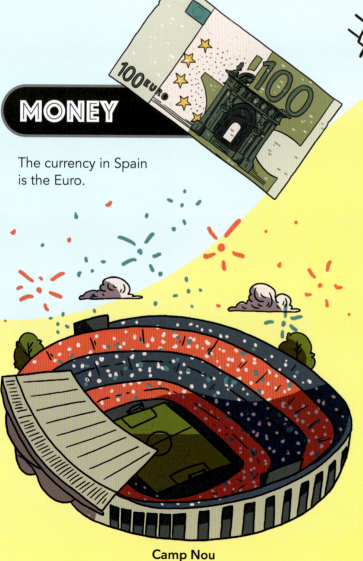

Camp Nou

FOOD

Paella

Paella is a traditional dish all over Spain but in Barcelona they love it made with fresh seafood.

Flavour bombs

Tapas are small plates of food. Look out for a giant potato croquette called 'la bomba' It's served with garlic sauce and spicy red sauce that explodes in your mouth like a flavour bomb!

Paella

La Bomba

La Rambla

PLACES TO GO

The Museu Picasso

The Spanish painter Pablo Picasso (1881-1973) lived and studied art in Barcelona as a young man. The Museu Picasso was opened in 1963 and has 4,000 of his works, including paintings from his Blue Period.

La Rambla

La Rambla is probably the most famous street in the city. No cars are allowed and people are free to mill around the many cafes and shops. This is a great place to grab an ice cream and watch the world go by!

The Palau de la Música Catalan

The Palau de la Música Catalan (the Music Palace) is a beautiful concert hall that was created by the Catalan architect Lluís Domènech i Montaner and opened in 1908. Today it is a UNESCO World Heritage Site hosting audiences at live music performances all year round.

25

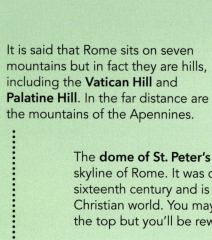

It is said that Rome sits on seven mountains but in fact they are hills, including the **Vatican Hill** and **Palatine Hill**. In the far distance are the mountains of the Apennines.

The **dome of St. Peter's Basilica**, in the Vatican, stands out on the skyline of Rome. It was designed by Michelangelo back in the sixteenth century and is considered one of the holiest churches in the Christian world. You may get out of breath climbing the 551 steps to the top but you'll be rewarded with breathtaking views of the city.

In the middle of Rome stands the mighty **Colosseum** (the Flavian Amphitheatre), one of the biggest amphitheatres in the world. It was constructed around 70-80 CE and is wearing well considering its age. In ancient times, people watched gladiator fights, executions and dramas here. Today it is one of the world's most popular tourist attractions.

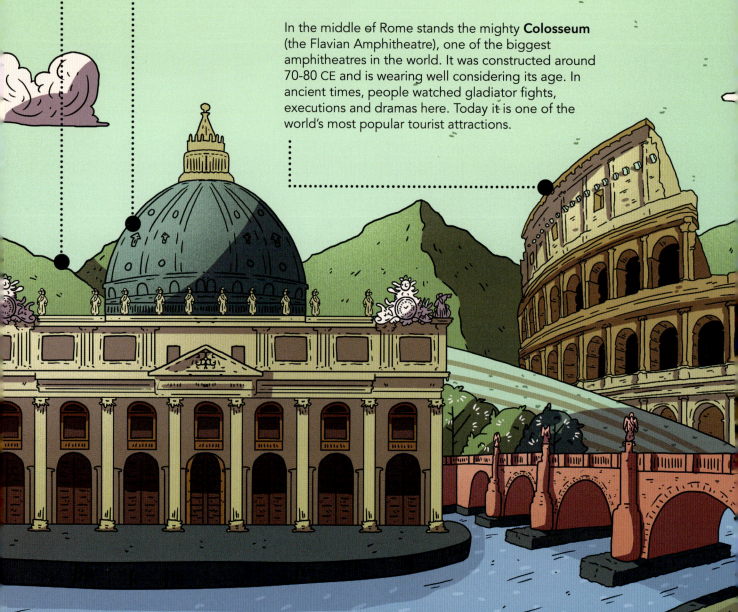

The Tiber River flows through Rome and many old bridges cross the famous ancient waterway. One of the most famous is the Ponte Sant'Angelo, with its statues of saints and angels. You can get a good view of St. Peter's Basilica from this bridge too.

ROME

ITALY

Ciao! Welcome to Rome, the busy and beautiful capital of Italy. It has around 2.9 million inhabitants and welcomes millions of tourists every year. The best way to see this city is on foot and around every corner you'll see something wonderful. It is famous for its ancient and classical architecture, grand squares, gardens, fountains, statues and delicious food – no wonder it's the third most visited city in Europe.

There are only a few skyscrapers in Rome. The tallest is **Torre Eurosky**, a residential tower which stands at 120 m.

The **Pantheon** is a temple built by the Romans around 120 CE. Its giant dome has a diameter of 43 m and is the largest unsupported dome in the world.

HISTORY

The saying 'Rome wasn't built in a day' is quite true. It's taken thousands of years for this famous city to evolve from a settlement on the Tiber River. One story is that is was founded in 713 BCE by the first king of Rome, Romulus. Later, Rome became the centre of the mighty Roman Empire and at one time was the largest city in the world. When the Empire collapsed, Rome declined too. The city bounced back when the Pope was in charge. During the Renaissance it was a centre for art and culture. It was made the capital of Italy in 1871 and has been described as the 'Eternal City'.

Lupa Capitolina statue

MONEY

In Italy, the local currency is the Euro. Make sure you take plenty of coins to throw into the many fountains!

PLACES TO GO

Roman Forum

Soak up the history of ancient Rome at the Roman Forum. Once upon a time, this was the centre of the city. Today, you can explore the ruins of temples and government buildings at the site.

Palatine Hill

Romulus is said to have founded the city on the Palatine Hill. Now it is a lovely green space and one of the most peaceful places in the city.

Vatican City

Vatican City is the world's smallest country. Walled off within the city of Rome, it has a population of around 1,000 people and is ruled by the head of the Catholic Church – the Pope.

Vatican City is a special place for Roman Catholics as it's the official residence of the Pope. It also has some magnificent holy buildings and museums. The highlight for many people is the Sistine Chapel with its awesome ceiling paintings by Michelangelo.

Vatican City

FOOD

Pizza

In Rome they like to eat dinner late at night – around 8 to 9 pm in the week and ten o' clock at the weekend. You will find pasta and pizza everywhere, but in Rome the speciality is thin-crust pizzas that just melt in your mouth.

Ice cream

Rome prides itself on having the best selection of ice cream (gelato) of probably any capital city. Many of the ices are made with fresh fruit, nuts and natural flavours – and eating them is one of the best ways to cool down on a hot and sticky day.

Nasoni

In the summertime Rome is very hot, so you need to drink lots of water. Look out for small water fountains called 'nasoni' ('big noses').

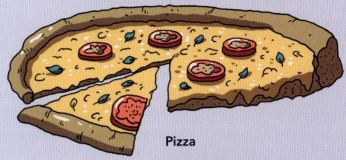

Pizza

Ice cream

Bocca della Verita

THINGS TO DO

Throw a coin in the Trevi Fountain

If you want to return to Rome again one day, then legend says you should throw a coin in the famous Trevi Fountain. It may sound like a silly idea but around 3,000 Euros are thrown into the fountain every day. This money is used to feed homeless people in Rome.

Put your hand in the Bocca della Verità

Do you dare to place your hand in the Bocca della Verità (Mouth of Fate) at the entrance to the Santa Maria in Cosmedin Church. It is said that, if you have told a lie it will bite your hand off!

29

Athens is surrounded by mountains and built on hills. **Mount Lycabettus** is within the city and at 277 m high is one of the best places to get a fabulous view over all of Athens. If you walk up to the top you may just find a wild Greek tortoise – some of which are over 100 years old!

Built on a great, rocky hill around 2,500 years ago, the **Acropolis** is a collection of ancient buildings, including gateways, temples and theatres – many of which are just ruins today.

The **Parthenon** is the most famous building on the Acropolis. It is a temple dedicated to Athena, the ancient goddess and patron of the city. A temple has stood here since 447 BCE. The giant columns are made from limestone and were once topped with carvings telling stories about the ancient Greek gods. The original carvings from the Parthenon were taken to London, Paris and Denmark in the nineteenth century. Greece would like these carvings back!

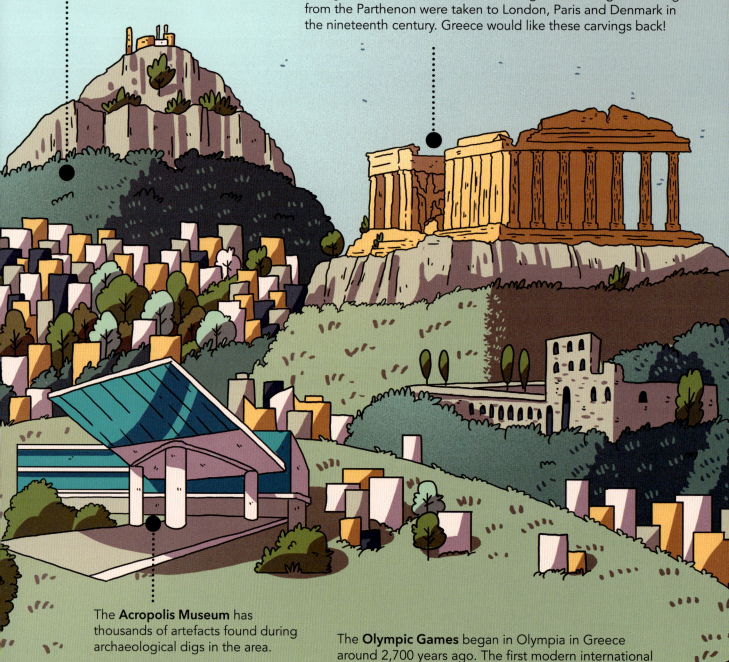

The **Acropolis Museum** has thousands of artefacts found during archaeological digs in the area.

The **Olympic Games** began in Olympia in Greece around 2,700 years ago. The first modern international Olympic Games were held in Athens in 1896. In 2004 the Games returned to the city with many of the events taking place at the Spyros Louis Stadium.

ATHENS
GREECE

Yasou (hello) from Athens, the capital city of Greece. Nearly everywhere you go here, you can look up and see the magnificent Parthenon. It has stood guard over the city for over 2,000 years. Today, the city is home to around 3.8 million people, making it the sixth most populated capital in Europe. It's busy and in the summer it's very hot, but this city is alive with history, art, culture, food and dancing.

Athenians are proud of the Parthenon and no skyscrapers have been allowed in the central city because they would ruin the view of the building. **Athens Tower** is 103 m and the tallest building in the city.

The beautiful **Metropolitan Cathedral** was built between 1842 and 1862, after Greece gained independence from the Ottoman Empire in 1832. The cathedral's interior is adorned with gold.

The port of **Piraeus** is one of the busiest ports in the world and it's full of holiday-makers catching ferries to the Greek islands. Piraeus is a city too – just 10 km away from the centre of Athens.

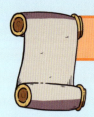

HISTORY

Athens is one of the oldest cities in the world with history and myths that go back around 5,000 years. Athens got its name from ancient Greek mythology as it was named after the goddess of wisdom, Athena. The city was the centre of politics, culture and the arts throughout Greek and Roman times. In 1458 Athens was invaded by the Ottoman Turks and the famous Parthenon was made into a mosque. In 1834, Athens was declared the capital of the newly-independent Greece.

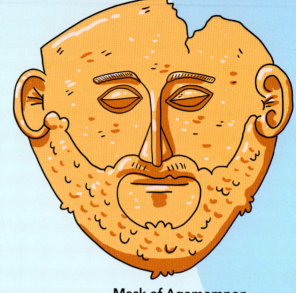

Mask of Agamemnon

MONEY

Ancient Greece was one of the first civilisations to use coins as money. The Euro is now the official currency in Greece.

PLACES TO GO

The National Archaeological Museum

Athens is an archaeologist's dream and millions of artefacts have been unearthed in this city. The National Archaeological Museum is home to the ancient Artemision Bronze (below left). This famous sculpture could be either Zeus or Poseidon – it is mighty, powerful and has no eyes, so it looks a bit scary. This museum also has the Golden Mask of Agamemnon (above) which dates back to 1,500 BCE, but shines so brightly it could have been made yesterday.

The National Gardens

The National Gardens is the perfect place to escape the crowded streets, museums and historic landmarks. This green park was built in 1838 by the first queen of Greece, Queen Amalia. There are shady walkways, ponds and a zoo.

Theatre of Dionysus Eleuthereus

The Theatre of Dionysus Eleuthereus was built in the fourth century BCE and is believed to be the oldest theatre in the world. Back then it could hold 17,000 people who came here to see plays by famous Greek playwrights including Sophocles, Euripides and Aeschylus.

Artemision Bronze

FOOD

Meze

Greek food is very popular internationally, so you may already know about dishes such as humus and taramasalata. In Athens the tavernas serve these and other small starter dishes called *meze*.

Dolmades

Dolmades are vine leaves stuffed with rice.

Tzatziki

Tzatziki is a cucumber dip that goes well with aubergines. Greeks love aubergines and they are used all the time, whether stuffed, fried, turned into dips or layered with meat or vegetable sauce in moussaka!

Loukoumades

A real sweet treat are fluffy fried doughnuts called loukoumades. They are usually served with honey and cinnamon and they just melt in your mouth.

Dolmades

Loukoumades

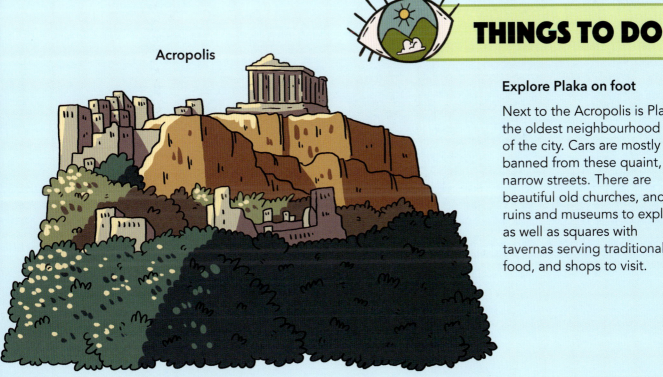

Acropolis

THINGS TO DO

Explore Plaka on foot

Next to the Acropolis is Plaka, the oldest neighbourhood of the city. Cars are mostly banned from these quaint, narrow streets. There are beautiful old churches, ancient ruins and museums to explore, as well as squares with tavernas serving traditional food, and shops to visit.

Istanbul was sometimes called **New Rome** and like Rome it was built on seven hills. Today each of the hills has its own mosque.

In 2019, **Çamlıca Mosque** was opened on Çamlıca Hill. It is the largest mosque in Turkey and can hold 63,000 people.

Galata Tower has been watching over the city since medieval times. This stone tower is 66.9 m high and if you visit the cafe on the upper floors you'll get an awesome view over the city.

Istanbul has two of the most magnificent buildings in the world and they are less than two km from each other. Just a few minutes' walk from the Hagia Sophia is the **Blue Mosque** (Sultan Ahmed Mosque). It was built between 1609 and 1616.

The **Hagia Sophia** was one of the seven wonders of the medieval world. The 55-m dome that spans the main building was considered a work of genius when it was constructed in 532 CE. The building has served as a church and a mosque but has been a museum since 1935.

ISTANBUL
TURKEY

Merhaba! Welcome to Istanbul, where two continents meet and the East greets the West. The Bosphorus is a waterway that runs north-south through the city dividing it into the European side (*Avrupa Yakası*) and the Asian side (*Anadolu Yakası*). With a population of over 15 million, Istanbul is the biggest city in Europe, but it isn't the capital of Turkey – Ankara is. Istanbul has an unforgettable skyline filled with domes and minarets. It is a city that never sleeps, with friendly people ready to welcome you.

The skyline of Istanbul is filled with historic buildings but skyscrapers are popping up all the time. Now Istanbul has the second highest number of skyscrapers over 100 m tall, of any European city. The **Metropol Istanbul** has three towers with the tallest at around 300 m, making it the tallest building in the city to date.

The **Golden Horn** is a freshwater estuary that served as a harbour for Istanbul in the past. It gets its name from the colour of the water at sunset.

Overlooking the Golden Horn stands **Topkapı Palace**. It was built between 1466 and 1478 as a residence for the Ottoman sultans. The palace was used for over 400 years with successive sultans adding their own halls and pavilions. At one time there were 5,000 people living within its walls.

The **Galata Bridge** which crosses the Golden Horn is one of the famous landmarks of the city.

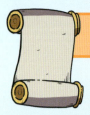

HISTORY

The skyline of Istanbul reveals its long and fascinating history. Many of those towers, domes and minarets were built during Byzantine (330-1453) or Ottoman (1453-1922) times. However, the history of the city goes back to the ancient Greeks who founded the settlement around 660 BCE and called it Byzantium. Later, under the Romans, it was called Constantinople. As Constantinople it became the capital of the Ottoman Empire and the centre of trade between the East and West. After the Turkish War of Independence in 1923 the capital of Turkey was switched to Ankara and Constantinople was renamed Istanbul.

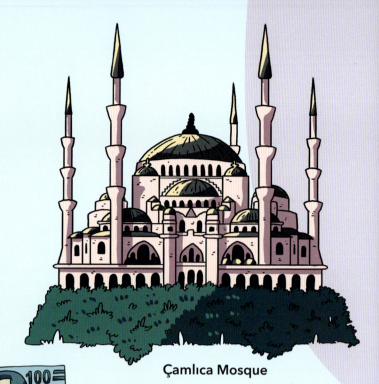

Çamlıca Mosque

MONEY

The currency in Istanbul is the Turkish Lira.

PLACES TO GO

Basilica Cistern

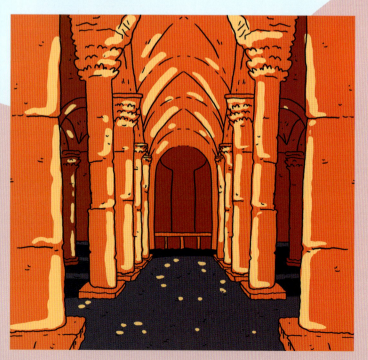

Basilica Cistern

Basilica Cistern

You need to go underground to see the Basilica Cistern which was built in early Roman times around 1,500 years ago. It's amazing to think that something so beautiful which looks more like a cathedral was used to filter water. The ceiling of the chamber is supported by 336 columns. Once this chamber was filled with water but now there is just enough water for a few carp to swim in.

Blue Mosque

To understand why the Blue Mosque gets its name you need to step inside. Look up at all the gorgeous blue tiles that cover the walls and domes. At night, the light turns blue as it is filtered through the stained glass windows. This is an active mosque which means there are prayer services here every day, and you have to take your shoes off at the entrance.

FOOD

ISTANBUL
TURKEY

Doner kebab

Turkish meals are packed with fresh vegetables. However, this is also the home of the meaty doner kebab and you'll find them being sold on every street corner! There are all kinds of kebabs to be found in Istanbul – meat is minced with seeds, nuts and vegetables to create some of the tastiest fast food ever!

Something sweet

If you have a sweet tooth then Turkish delight (also called *lokum*) and baklava are for you! Turkish delight is a sweet with a jelly-like texture that is flavoured with rosewater – nuts and fruits are sometimes added too. Baklava is made from filo pastry and nuts drenched in honey or syrup.

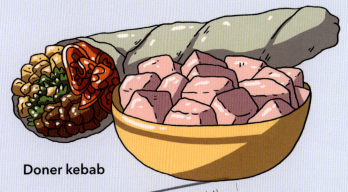

Doner kebab

Turkish delight

THINGS TO DO

Travel along the Bosphorus

Sit back and enjoy the view of the city as you travel along the Bosphorus. You literally change continents as the ferry or river cruiser travels through the Bosphorus Strait and takes you from Asia to Europe.

Shop in the Grand Bazaar

Get lost in time and place at Istanbul's Grand Bazaar. This enormous market dates back to medieval times and has 61 streets and 4,000 or more shops. Spices, jewellery, rugs and leather goods are just a few of the tempting things on sale here!

Bosphorus

The observation deck of the **A'DAM Tower** offers the best views of the city. If you're feeling brave you can try 'Over the Edge' which is Europe's highest swing. Imagine the thrill of swinging at 100 m in the air, from the edge of the tower!

Westerkerk Tower is the highest church tower in the city. Its bright blue and gold dome has been part of skyline since 1631.

Dam Square is the historical heart of Amsterdam, with shops, restaurants and cafes galore. It's always full of life and action. On national holidays, such as *Koningsdag* or King's Day, there are massive celebrations here.

Overlooking **Dam Square**, is the beautiful **Royal Palace** built for the royal family in the seventeenth century. These days, the royals only use it about once a year which means it is often open to the public.

There's water, water everywhere in this city. The **Amstel River** connects to a network of canals and the large waterfront called the **IJ**. One of the best ways of seeing Amsterdam is by glass-topped ferry.

AMSTERDAM

NETHERLANDS

Welkom to Amsterdam, the capital of the Netherlands. You're going to see a lot of canals, flowers and bicycles in this pretty place. The city of Amsterdam has a population of under a million so it feels more relaxed than many other capitals. It's also flat and compact so it's easy to see everything either by foot or by bike.

Amsterdam has over 100 km of canals and many of these were built in the seventeenth century. The **Brouwersgracht** is one of the prettiest canals in old Amsterdam. It gets its name from the breweries that were built in the area. There are lots of beautiful old buildings and bridges to see on a stroll along the canal paths.

The **Port of Amsterdam** is the fourth busiest in Europe for cargo and the largest port for cocoa in the world. It stands on the banks of the North Sea Canal which connects it to the North Sea.

The **Oude Kerk** is the oldest building in the city. Built in the thirteenth century it was a church for over 800 years and is now a museum.

At 26.6 m, **De Gooyer** is the tallest wooden windmill in the Netherlands. The original mill dates from the sixteenth century, but this version was restored in the 1920s.

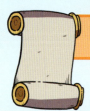

HISTORY

Amsterdam gets its name from the dam on the Amstel River on which it grew back in the twelfth century. This is a city literally built on water, with some parts of Amsterdam 4 m below sea level. Through the centuries a system of dykes, canals and barrages were built to stop the water. By the seventeenth century, Amsterdam was the centre of trade and the richest city in the world. Since then the city has seen war, recession and recovery. Today, it is one of the most popular tourist destinations in Europe and a centre for business and finance.

MONEY

The Euro is the currency used in Amsterdam.

PLACES TO GO

Anne Frank House

It's hard not to feel sad when you visit the Anne Frank House. During the Second World War, Anne and her family hid from the Nazis in this house. Anne wrote about the experience in a diary which was published as *The Diary of a Young Girl* and became an international bestseller. Anne never knew that she would become so famous because she died, aged 15, in a Nazi concentration camp. You can visit the rooms where Anne and her family lived during her brief teenage years.

Van Gogh Museum

The Van Gogh Museum displays the biggest collection of Vincent Van Gogh's works in the world. There are over 200 of his paintings and 500 drawings. Get up close and see the colours and brushstrokes that he used for his masterpieces, including *Sunflowers* and *Almond Blossom*.

The Starry Night by Vincent van Gogh

FOOD

Stroopwafels

The waffles in Amsterdam are best served hot and gooey. Stroopwafels are waffles glued together with syrup and they are a chewy delight!

Fresh fish

Amsterdam is near the North Sea and fresh cod or whiting are very popular. *Kibbeling* and *lekkerbek* are battered white fried fish, served with mayonnaise.

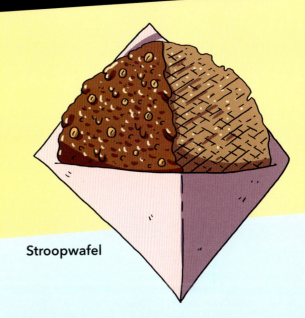

Stroopwafel

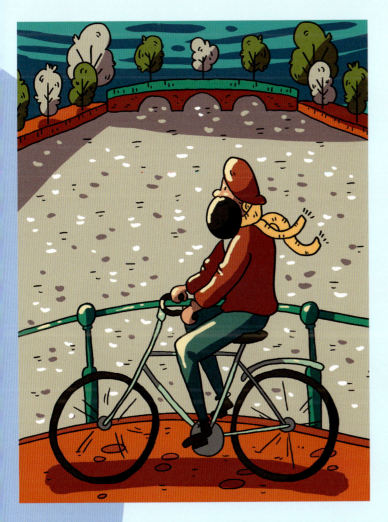

THINGS TO DO

Hire a bike and go for a ride

With over 400 km of cycle paths Amsterdam is a paradise for cyclists. It's easy to hire a bike and there are plenty of green spaces and canal paths to explore. Vondelpark is the largest park in the city with lovely ponds and lakes to cycle around. Look out for *The Fish* sculpture by Picasso and the wild parakeets that squawk in the trees!

You can enjoy a lovely view of the city from Stockholm's highest hill called **Skinnarviksberget**. There are no modern high rises in the centre so it truly is a cityscape like no other!

Where there is water there are bridges and viaducts. In Stockholm there are 57 bridges. **Västerbron** (the West Bridge) spans 600 m. It's a great place to look across to **Gamla Stan** (the old town).

A walk through the cobbled streets of **Gamla Stan** is like a stroll back to medieval times. Some of the buildings date back to the thirteenth century. **Stortorget** (Grand Square) is the oldest square in the city and it looks especially pretty when the Christmas market is set up each year.

The **Ericsson Globe** is an extraordinary space-age-looking building. It's the largest spherical building in the world. It opened in 1989 and is mostly used as a venue for ice hockey matches. It also represents the Sun in Sweden's largest scale model of the solar system. The 'Earth' is 7,600 m away in the Swedish Museum of Natural History.

Storkyrkan (Stockholm Cathedral) is another building in the Old Town that has survived since medieval times.

The **Royal Palace** is the official residence of the Swedish royal family. It was built in the eighteenth century and it's bigger than most other palaces in Europe. Look out for the changing of the royal guard.

STOCKHOLM
SWEDEN

Hej from Stockholm, the capital of Sweden. You're never far away from the water here as the city is built across 14 islands. Lake Mälaren is to the west and the Baltic Sea is to the east. It's the biggest city in Scandinavia with a population of nearly 1 million. There are historical quarters, old palaces, parks and even beaches to explore in this happy Scandi capital.

Kista is a modern part of the city where many businesses are located. **Kista Science City** is the largest Information and Communications Technology cluster in Europe so it often gets called the 'Silicon Valley of Europe'. Kista Science Tower and the Victoria Tower are two of Amsterdam's tallest buildings.

Stockholm City Hall is built from 8 million bricks and features a spire with three golden crowns. Every year the internationally famous Nobel Prize Award Ceremony and Banquet takes place here. The evening ends with dancing in the Golden Hall which sparkles with over 18 million gold tiles.

HISTORY

Stockholm started as a village on Lake Mälaren back in the thirteenth century. It quickly developed into the largest city in Sweden. Over the centuries, the city has been ravaged by fire, invaded by enemy powers and struck down with the plague. Amazingly, it still has one of the best preserved old quarters of any city in Europe. However, since the Second World War the city has been modernised and it is now one of the most eco-friendly, forward-thinking places in the world.

Vasa

MONEY

One day, Stockholm aims to become cashless and have people use cards only. For now you will need Swedish Krona coins and bank notes to spend.

PLACES TO GO

The Vasa Museum

Ship Ahoy! The Vasa Museum is home to the most incredibly well-preserved seventeenth-century ship. Three hundred years ago the Vasa sank in the waters off Stockholm. It was raised in 1961 and today you can see the restored version (above). Over 95 per cent of the ship is original, including the carved sculptures that decorate the outside.

Iron Boy

When you're in Gamla Stan (Old Town) see if you can find Stockholm's smallest statue. 'Iron Boy' or 'little boy who looks at the moon' is about 15 centimetres high and stands in the backyard of the Finnish Church. In winter he wears a hat and scarf.

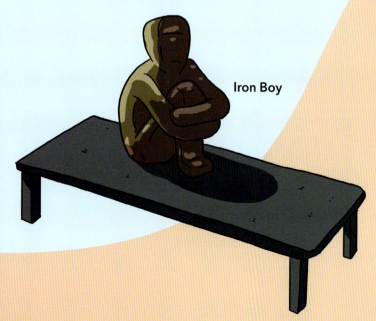

Iron Boy

FOOD

Coffee and cake

In Stockholm you will hear people talk about *fika* which means coffee and cake. Traditional fika always includes little cinnamon buns called *kanelbullar*.

Meatballs

Swedes love their meatballs or *köttbullar*. Traditional meatballs are made from veal and served with mashed potatoes and lingonberry sauce.

Kanelbullar

Köttbullar

THINGS TO DO

Ride the Stockholm Metro

The Stockholm Metro is the quickest way to get across this city. However, you may get delayed looking at all the amazing sculptures, paintings and mosaics on display. There are 100 stations on the network and most of these are decorated with works of art dating from the 1950s to the present day.

Visit Djurgården Island

Djurgården Island was once a royal hunting park but today it is a special place that anyone can visit. It is a lovely green space but also has fun fairs, a zoo and a museum devoted to the pop group ABBA.

ABBA

MORE EUROPEAN CITIES

PRAGUE

Everywhere you look in Prague, the capital of the Czech Republic, you'll see incredible old buildings. Beautiful examples of medieval and art nouveau architecture are everywhere! It's known as the 'City of a Hundred Spires' because of its many turrets and church towers. You'll see lots of Gothic gargoyles staring down at you, too!

Population: 1.3 million

Highest building: Žižkov Television Tower 216 m

Places to see: Charles Bridge, Old Town Square, Prague Castle, Vitus Cathedral

VIENNA

Austria's capital is also known as the 'Capital City of Music' because of its links to classical composers including Beethoven, Brahms and Haydn. This is a city filled with history, culture and grand buildings. The psychoanalyst Sigmund Freud and artist Gustav Klimt lived here.

Population: 1.9 million (2018)

Highest building: DC Towers 220 m

Places to see: The Hofburg, St. Stephen's Cathedral, Belvedere Palace, Leopold Museum

REYKJAVÍK

The capital city of Iceland is the most northerly capital in the world and when you look around you and see snow-capped mountains it really feels it! Reykjavík is small but it has a massive reputation for being clean, green and safe as well as having interesting architecture and a lively art and music scene. Take note; it is one of the most expensive cities in Europe!

Population: 128,793 (2019)

Highest building: Hallgrímskirkja 74.5 m

Places to see: Hallgrímskirkja (cathedral), Harpa Concert Hall and Conference Centre, Perlan

ZURICH

The largest city in Switzerland is famous for its picturesque old town as well as its financial institutions and banks. In recent years it has become a fashionable cultural centre too. Situated beside Lake Zurich, this pretty city often tops the lists for the best place to live in the world.

Population: 415,215 (2018)

Highest building: Prime Tower 126 m

Places to see: Fraumünster (Woman's Church), Lindenhof, Schweizerisches Landesmuseum (Swiss National Museum), Zurich Zoo

WARSAW

The capital city of Poland was once considered so beautiful it was called 'the Paris of the North'. The city was devastated in the Second World War with around 85 per cent of its buildings lost. It still has some historical landmarks, especially in the Old Town, but now Warsaw has a modern skyline packed with skyscrapers.

Population: 1.78 million

Highest building: Palace of Culture and Science 237 m

Places to see: Old Town, Presidential Palace, Royal Castle, Łazienki Park, Palace of Culture and Science

LISBON

The capital of Portugal is one of the oldest cities in the world with evidence of people living there from around the eighth century BCE. The city is located on the mouth of the Tagus River and nestled within seven hills. Explore the cobbled streets and you'll discover ancient castles and churches, monasteries and more.

Population: 505,526 (2017)

Highest building: Monsanto Tower 120 m

Places to see: Mosteiro dos Jerónimos (monastery), Castelo de São Jorge (castle), Praça do Comércio (Commercial Square)

COPENHAGEN

Enter one of the greenest cities in the world! Copenhagen is the capital of Denmark and the best way to get around is by bike. Cycle around its cobbled streets, see the pretty, brightly-coloured houses and take in the City Hall, palaces, squares and Victorian gardens. The waterways are so clean you can even take a swim. Most of the shopping takes place in Strøget, one of Europe's longest pedestrianised streets. Denmark is the home of LEGO so this is a great place to pick some up!

Population: 777,218 (2018)

Highest building: Herlev Hospital 120 m

Places to see: Frederiksberg Palace, Tivoli Gardens, The Little Mermaid, Nyhavn

EDINBURGH

Look down from the turrets of Edinburgh Castle and you'll get a magnificent view of the Scottish capital. From the cobbled streets of the Old Town below, across to the Royal Mile with its shops and galleries, ahead to the New Town with its rows of grand eighteenth-century houses and beyond to the beaches at Portobello. No wonder it is often named one of the best places to live in the world!

Population: 518,500 (2018)

Highest building: St Mary's Episcopal Cathedral 90 m

Places to see: Edinburgh Castle, Scott Monument, Palace of Holyroodhouse, Arthur's Seat

GLOSSARY

barrage
an artificial barrier that prevents flooding.

communist
someone who believes that all property should be owned by the community and not by private individuals.

couture
the design and making of high-end clothing.

dyke
a wall that prevents flooding.

embalmed
preserved after death.

Gothic
describes a type of architecture from the twelfth to the sixteenth century used to build many churches and cathedrals.

iconic
describes something famous or very easily recognised.

landmarks
features of a place that are easily recognised.

liberation
the act of setting someone or something free.

medieval
related to the Middle Ages (fifth to the fifteenth century).

minaret
a tower on a mosque.

Modernist
descibes buildings designed to be made with new materials, such as steel and concrete, rather than styled in a more ornate, traditional way.

mosaic
a picture created by using small pieces of stone or glass to make a bigger image or pattern.

Nobel Prize
one of six annual prizes awarded in categories ranging from physics to literature to peace.

occupation
a job.

revolution
the overthrow of a government.

taverna
a small restaurant in Greece.

INDEX